For: DARIUS and
ANITA
———— with wishes for
good reading with
WOMAN TALKING WOMAN !

Maxine Tynes
24/11/90

Woman Talking Woman

Maxine Tynes

Pottersfield Press
Lawrencetown Beach, Nova Scotia
Canada

For All The Sisters.

Copyright 1990 Maxine Tynes

Front cover painting by Rosemary McDonald (photo by Albert Lee)

Back cover photo: Shirley Robb

Canadian Cataloguing in Publication Data

Tynes, Maxine

Woman talking woman

ISBN 0-919001-64-5

I. Title

**PS8589.Y53W65 1990   C811'.54   C90-097627-6
PR9199.3.T96W65 1990**

Published with the Assistance of The Nova Scotia Department of Tourism and Culture and The Canada Council

Pottersfield Press
RR 2, Porters Lake
Nova Scotia B0J 2S0
Canada

Contents

AS THE BOOK BEGINS
On publishing my first collection of poems.

as the book begins
as you read me now
as you turn my pages
as you look through my leaves
sample my thoughts
stack up my isms
walk through my present
my past
and my fantasy
measure the depth of my love
and time (for all time)
my moments of weakness
as you gauge, in turn
my humour
my candour
my wit
and my judgmental self
I stand hopeful and afraid, and
move over
and over and over your threshold
as the book begins
as you read me now.

WOZA MANDELA!

Woza Mandela!
Raise the fist, the heart
The mind of freedom
Raise the flag of the heart
Call up the young lions
Call up the ANC
Call up the UDF
Call up the Black Sash
Call up the women, the men
The children in the street
Call up the heart, the mind
The viscera of the world
To disembowel apartheid
To dismantle minority rule
To engage the rule of humanity
To dance Black unity in the streets of Soweto
In the streets of Sharpville
And of Uitenhague
To count the ribs of apartheid as they fall
To the streets of hell
To sing
To sing
To sing/shout/dance Mandela
As we raise up again
The phoenix of this Mandela man
Woza Mandela!
Woza Mandela!
Woza to the head of the lions of Black Africa.

I. Woman Talking Woman

ALL THE SISTERS

All the sisters in some parade
of the female side of things
trailing sister sibling memories
and rivalries and, the heroes
we were each, in turn,
for one another.
I wanted her handwriting;
You wanted the skirts and bracelets,
The shoes and colour of her.

I watched my little sisters listen
for the phone to ring and ring and
ring for me,
with some George or Mike or Glenn;
waiting for some-man-on-the-line
future rings of their own.
We all, in turn, watched and wanted
and tried on each other's style
and hair and lipstick-mouth in the mirror.
Now, each sister, here, under these August trees;
sitting and seeing and, saying we're o.k.

LIFE UP IN FLAMES

Life up in flames.
Mandela woman
you live on the edge of our world
hope drifts by on the wind
freedom drops from the sky
like rain on parched ground
there, then dried
then gone
leaving something on the air.
Life up in flames.
They eat and grow big on
the smoke of your kitchen
and your Nelson bedspring memories.
Mandela woman;
this sun we both rise to
will see my tears for you
and dry them as they drop
like rain, on a parched ground
there,
then dried,
then gone.

FOR THE MONTREAL FOURTEEN WHO LIVED AND DIED IN THE HEARTBEAT OF WOMAN

To add my voice to the community of women as we raise our hearts and our voices and our hands in this time of sorrow and of healing in December of 1989.

For every woman voice left in sorrow and in silence
for every woman breast left bruised and aching
for every woman eye left red and drowned in the well of tears

for every woman-place entered in anger
                    entered in pain
                    entered without mercy
                            without wanting
                            without love
                            without love

for every woman dream left shallow
for every woman hand in a fist of empty rage
                                  rage
                                  rage

for every woman-want denied
                    devalued
                    belittled
                    ignored
                    unanswered

for every woman body torn and bleeding
for every woman heart torn asunder
for every woman place hollow
                    bare
                    plundered
                    raped
                    bereft
                    and left wanting

We stand
and we shout
      weep
      shout
      testify

We raise the heart and hands of sorrow
                and of mourning
                and of healing
this womanist body politic.

NIGHTSONG

For the TAKE BACK THE NIGHT MARCH held in Halifax on October 9th, 1987

The night is a shadow of male intentions
holding myth and fear
and pain that is too, too real
for the children
the men
the women who live each day
and each night.

The boy-child learns to brave the night,
the girl-child learns to fear it.

And, through it all,
orchestrating all of our growing up years:
'Be home before dark!'
'Be careful of the dark'
'Never go out alone at night!'

That leitmotif of warning and awareness.

The night beckons with a voice
that is, at once, seductive and betraying.

The night is a time of magic and dancing
and trysting by moonlight
in glitter and glamour
in satin and silk
and the stiletto heels of nightlife —
a little night-music, perhaps.

The night speaks in a voice that is
at once, seductive and betraying
and demands payment in a bruise,
blood, and unwelcome penetration.

Every campus is mine, and I'll walk it!
Every path is mine,
and I'll stroll around, or picnic by day or by night.
Point Pleasant, are you listening?

Every alley and corner is mine, and I'll have it!
Every hospital ground blackened by nightshade,
Every road, every crossing is mine, and I'll walk it!

I will rattle Morris and Hollis, and North and South Commons
striding over and up that hill called Citadel
down Artz and Granville and Grafton and Sackville
down Maynard and Preston and Seymour and Russell
Spring Garden and Blowers and North Park and South Park.

Let me push back that shadow
that nightful, hurtful nightshade.
Let me enter it and fill it with my body, my name
my self that is woman and strong
and make it my own.

Let me fill the night with my face and my stride
and my new-found woman-self;
Let me rattle that block and that road
and that street-corner lamp-post nighttime urban battleground
with this ordinary woman-courage
as I
as we
TAKE BACK THE NIGHT!

DEATH WATCH
On the death of my mother, Ada Maxwell Tynes on June 20, 1987

grief enters, and
walks upright in this room,
imposes itself on this
company of strangers which is you, my family
here now
in this too public and ill-fitting death-watch chamber
around our mother.

the hollow weep and call of grief
sounds over and over in the cave of my heart;
my voice finds no sound to give it life
no tears to give it freedom.

this grief
begs at the corners of eyes for tears
and, finds some comfort in the flood
which spills, so willingly,
from the brothers' eyes.

ah, grief —
you'll find none here,
only that hollow and silent sound
which rings deep and deep
and deep and unyielding in the heart of love
bereft and incised and left wanting.

TO GIVE PAUSE
For my mother

Mum,
your death is an inconvenience to me, I think.
And, immediately I smile to think that the first and lingering
hours of my birth were the same for you;
not time
not ready
no warning
just as you are for me now,
lying cold and the same but different.

Everything inconveniences women:
birth
and life, insisting itself on us each robust month;
our bodies,
growing and shrinking and growing;
our hair, never right
our men, never quite what we had in mind.

My life can pause now, for you
as yours did, so profoundly,
to find me here.

CONTROL

Controlling the heavens of your smile in mine
I let down the rain
rain
rain
Of all the feeling harnessed there
within that smile —
yours,
all controlled moustache hair
licked and fingered just so
above that red and pouty lip or kiss or kiss
within that smile;
mine,
fulsome lips rolling back
escape of teeth and tongue
and rock and roll of laugh and laugh and laugh.
This, then, is the control I roll and run with
from smile
to full-tilt boogie laugh
from the gut, belly, down and down
somewhere
somewhere, where that laugh
becomes control out-of-control
becomes some love-rap
becomes some belly to belly number
that only lovers know the lyrics to.
This, then, is the control I roll and run with,
that I dance on
that I call my smile for you
that I sift through your moustache
and the stuff of your days to find
that I reach and call for
that invents and reinvents my time for you
and my heart
heart-beat
heart-beat
the one behind my smile
the one I control, out-of-control, for you.

TRIBUNAL

You are my tribunal
at the end of the long road
which is our togetherness
your eyes are judgement
they take the measure of
every word
     tear
     shout
     recrimination.

It is hard now to change these sheets,
to make up this judge, jury, witness-box bed
which single, double, king-and-queen-sized
we shared;
we tally and we tally
the thrust and parry of meal-time conversation;
there is no mercy here
the quality of, to be tempered
no appeal;
no one but you to be privy to this plea
so, I take the law into my own hands
I legalize all arguments with silence
I jury every glance of contempt and heartache
I police my thoughts of love for you
I seize the moment and tear your picture
but I will hear no verdict
no barrister will appeal my fate, or yours
I take the law into my own hands;
I give it a heart and soul
and I set it free.

THERE YOU STAND

Out of all of the yesterdays of beginnings
and all of the tomorrows of endings
and goodbyes,
there you stand
in the middle of my days and nights
and in the middle of my life
making stars and suns shine more brightly
happiness lasts longer
laughter sounds more deeply
a smile — yours, or mine for you,
is incandescent in the joy
it marks again and again
on this mirror of my love
and my longing for you.

There you stand
like a flag of all that love is
and all that love will be.
I look up and there you are
a banner on the winds
that buffet and change us
that make us come and go
that make us resist and roll in
each, the words, the hearts, the arms of each other
that splash me at midnight in your eyes.

Your eyes at midnight are the pool
and pond and ocean I will swim and drown in.
I furl this flag of love around my life.
I unfurl it in the face of doubt
and chance and change.
We banner it across our days
like some heaven.
We fall and fly under it
out of all the yesterdays, and
into all of the tomorrows
and endings and goodbyes.

WHO IS THAT WOMAN?

I see you,
standing, or sitting, or
moving to somewhere
I see you as you see me —
as some woman, somewhere.
I measure you.
I weigh the possibilities and the probabilities of your life,
so many variables and complexities:
children, no children
housework to juggle between a job and school
some night course in pottery or computers or Tai Chi
or
a housekeeper, calls to make and to receive;
appointments: the dentist, the grocer, the cleaner,
the gynECOLOGIST
or, an answering machine,
a shower to go to,
carpools, plastics-cosmetic-erotica-dinner parties,
the hairdresser,
a hospital visit to a sick-or-birthing friend;
or, a close and private life
behind closed doors
DO - NOT - DISTURB!
a man, or, some men in tow
to dress and to dine, dance, fight, shop, cuddle, work,
eat, sleep with
or, no man in your life.
I see you, and
measure you against myself
and my life.
Do you see as I do?
Do you love as deeply?
Do you need and want and
take the world in strides as long and
as wide and as impatient as my own?
Do you hurt as long and as often as I do?
Do you live in many selves and faces,
a different one for each time and place

and person in your life?
Do you sometimes feel eighty - eighty - eighty
and fall into your bed, all aches and pains,
at baby's hour; just before sundown?
No love-nest here;
just snuggling down, down and down
to embrace sleep.
Do you see me as I see you?
Wondering in how many ways our lives dovetail?
Who is that woman?

ARE WE HAVING FUN YET?/
HIGHWAY VACATION, 1985

rolling miles
black and dappled cows fill my window
I am delighted
with the green and gold
cornfield childhood picture-book
non-t.v. screen display
you cannot change the channel
only with miles and miles of sitting
and the big six horses under the hood
sipping and drinking every litre;
me
smiling to see the gold hairs on your arm beside me
the other arm growing black
and masquerading in the tan you all pursue and
chase like hounds,
sun-dogs to some mecca of brown skin;
me, silent in the miles that drug us.
I look from yours to mine
so pigment brown and so real;
you, still so unbelieving
when we compare tan lines.

Are we there yet?   I ask.
And are we having fun?

you're not, as I badger you
for stops for Coke
and to pee
and accuse you of losing us
on some autoroute in the bowels of New England

eating,
at first (from leaving home)
saving-money-on-the-trip resolutions
we hoard pennies,
becoming picnic hamper vegetarians
as golden arches and neon burgers roll by

but later, and later still
we mark the miles with junkfood and pizza
greasy frenchfries and
mile-high clubhouse specials
in Middle America diners
where the waitresses are always Betsy or Darlene
and know the locals on a
no menu required, first-name basis.

us
two baked and broiled travellers in a glass-topped sedan
rolling, rolling, rolling
into cool evening
somewhere
somewhere on some road
I touch your arm
thinking of tonight

and how I'll want you
and how my energy for passion
will be matched by your poor, frozen-to-the-wheel
road-weary body
and I think of how and where to bargain for it, and more.

you,
oblivious to all of my real
and fantasy wantings;
your eyes
oozing blacktop, and double yellow lines
the pupils like two black and bull's-eye B.B.s
stretched out in one long black telegraph line
from here to there.

you sing out car makes and
curses to stupid motorists.

I think of how this tourist trip
makes you like a boy again
playing Eros twice in these mornings
in someone else's bed.

every year, it's the same thing
rolling away and back again
our eyes and skins and hearts and souls
snapping up shots of everywhere
like two whole-body Kodaks.

Are we having fun yet?   And,
Did we love it?
Did we want it?
Did we yell and scream for more?

CASHIERS AT THE SUPERMARKET

Cashiers never look into your eyes.
They fondle and trade someone else's cash
for tomatoes and cauliflower.
They see your fingers flashing nail polish, and
dirt from the field and factory
and the computer bank,
dropping, passing coins and dollars;
dollar bills, like lettuce, flutter and fall
hand to hand.
No eyes meet.
Woman at the register,
I want to see your eyes;
I want to see your youth and age.
I want to see your life in them.
Pass me my coins and cabbages
and a smile in your eyes;
or, the flicker of pain up from
eight hour legs
as the register clicks and beeps
and rings up our connection
at the check-out.

SOME ROMANTIC NOTION

Some romantic notion lifts you up
and carries you to somewhere
and, to everywhere;
Carries you to the mirror
to see the you who is not there
to see the you who is strong
and tall and wiser than
beautiful hair, perfect teeth,
and someone else's waistline;
Carries you to the street
that you walk with legs and feet
that move in a language that says:
You own the street!
I own the street!
Carries you into your life,
into your family's eyes to show
them that you are them but also, really you;
Carries you into some lovers' eyes and arms
to be all and whole and real in your
loving and giving woman to man to womanliness;
To look some romantic notion in the eye, and
in the heart and be it until it is you.

THIS WOMAN

This woman walks the world
my path is broad and narrow
my path is the way of
the mothers and sisters and daughters
of the world.
I take the steps of
woman, man, and
woman and man together;
my strides are passion and
pain and pleasure;
my steps are wonder and joy,
discovery and
the anger that builds and breaks
and bridges troubled times.
My arms swing wide to embrace
all that is warm and welcoming.
I yield and I give and I love.
My eyes sweep wide
this velvet-brown vision.
Through this eye darkly,
I take the measure of
this woman in this world

I AM

I am a woman who wears
elephants in her ears tonight
and, a blue-green parrot over her heart;
the rayon jungle flares and flutters
in Gauguin splendour across my breasts
and back.
In this room of art and culture,
I soar and fly in splendour and colours of
midnight and lapis and the sun,
while all around me,
the beige, blue, grey, grey, grey ones
fall away,
consumed by walls
and the night-time horizon.

WHAT I REALLY AM

I laugh into the mirror
and, up my sleeve
at the ruse I work and play
for daytime and public credibility.
This strong woman that I am
chanting lessons and poems at my students,
chanting isms and spirit in my political woman-self
for other political/non-political women and men.
But when night comes
or on some odd day-time moment
or moments, when you
and thoughts of you and me
invade my mind
relentlessly graphic and touch-real
then, to me, I am what I really am;
And always, and ever, am:
a woman lost in the jigsaw-puzzle dream of
you gone
and gone and me
still here
stupid and reeling in that daze
that won't go away
and that has me seeing you, still,
around every corner.

BEING

Being real and whole and bodyful;
turning pages,
greeting women who are flat and
glossy, magazine-slim and
dressed to kill budgets and men's eyes;
women with rainbow magazine eyes
breasts of a perfect no-size
with hips to match;
hands that spread wings and
fly in colours like birds,
and feet that perch and point
in heels and leather, or
perfect pink and brown barefoot footprints
in some Caribbean sand.

Being real and whole and bodyful;
with big hips and breast and belly,
filling rooms and other eyes
with this image
which does not slip across a glossy page
full of staples and designer fantasy.

THIS FIRST DAY OF SEPTEMBER

This first day of September
this sad-filled happy golden
September day.
The memory of August heat lingers,
and is gone;
the memory of all those golden leaves
of childhood's autumns, come and gone;
the ghost of little girl legs
one knee sock up,
one crinkled down
swishing through leaves
leaves
leaves
finding acorns and horse chestnuts
biting sour through green prickles
licking the brown silk nut-shine
hoarding horse chestnut bulges
in pocket, pocket, pocket —
swishing,
red, brown, gold-gold oak maple leaves
swishing, crunching, crackling
under these September feet.
All my red-gold sad and happy memories
this sad-filled happy golden September day.

SEA AND SKY

Some South Shore Maritime sometime
free from the city of everything
the road is soft and high and low
and endless in its route of
trees and sky.

I am not the driver.
I loll my head and dream
tires whisper whisper sand
beach sand
nosing the wind, so fresh from the sea,
like a hound.

I am the hound hanging from every car en route.

tongue out
panting time to rolling wheels and
beating dog-heart
ears painted back by the airstream.

Then the earth becomes the sky
those Atlantic blues and greys mesh
and, who can tell,
over and over the trees and endless road
Which is sea? Which is sky?
Will I, in this car, go plunging or flying?
Do I even care?

ENAMOURED OF THE BLACK AND WHITE COW

black and white
sweet graphic lady of the Vermont,
Quebec and Nova Scotia meadows.
Lady-cow,
so black-and-white surreal
and perfect against the sky
green grass, and,
through my car window
I am enamoured of your image
cow-magic before me.

Who paints your broad and angled back
and neck
and face
and breast, so dappled black and white
and perfect?

You roll your big and soft brown eyes.
I roll mine over you.

Your flick of tail
reveals the milk-bulk
sack of pink, pink udder;
I want to reach and heft
and stroke the weight
of pink and soft sweet
cow teat
      teat
      teat
      teat;
to nuzzle the wet and velvet of your nose,
to snuffle in the sweet
black and white cow scent of you,
sweet Bessie, Bossy, Violet or Moo.

You delicately tongue your cud
and let a long and rolling sigh
and settle into a graphic landscape with your sisters —

a black and white blanket titled:
   Holstein On a Vermont Hillside.
My car rolls by.
You are gone.

CROWS

Crows calling beyond the conference room,

Rusty night-black wings defying
the frigid day
gleaming beaks calling
and calling
beyond the window.
An acrobat among the frozen trees
as this verbal acrobatic academic afternoon
is here, and going on
and on.
Across the conference template
we swoop and call to each other
without the bold and elastic courage
of those crows which play and swoop and dip
and call and call.

Crows calling beyond the conference room.
Are these Dalhousie crows because
they swoop and call here?
Are they alter ego academe en wing?
En route? En flight?
Are they Lord of Dalhousie?
Are they Henry Hicks in flight?

They call and swoop and dodge frozen trees
and icy rooftops.
We palaver and swoop and dodge Dalhousie mission
and policy and change.

The call of raucous crows, heard and caught mid
frozen flight is
black and bright and bold
with feathers and passion
and the bawdy free-fall through frozen, frozen sky.

CROW POEM #2

And now you sit silently
Black puffs in the trees
Feathered punctuation
At the ends of branches.

SILENT CROWS

And now your feathered night-blackness is gone
freeing branches to the light and
to the weightlessness of day.
Without you,
without your black punctuation
the sky, the trees have no endpoint.
My eyes dart and dart
and, finding no crow-blackness,
wait for the night.

RICK HANSON: 1100 METRES HIGH IN HINTON, ALBERTA ON MARCH 20, 1987.

Rick Hanson crosses his last border today
leaving me,
and all of us, behind in
Halifax
St. John's
Windsor
Montreal
and everywhere;
to gripe about the snow
which keeps falling
and cold coffee;
red tape over taxes
and long lines at the cinema;
the Angus L. MacDonald toll booth,
and at the supermarket.
Rick Hansen crosses his last border today
and it's snowing in Hinton, Alberta.
I saw him on my C.B.C. MIDDAY T.V. screen
and I measured his speed against a hooting, hooting
blue and yellow VIA RAIL eastbound beside him.
It made for great T.V. visuals,
all that blue and yellow
and rolling wheelchair wheels
wheeling;
Hanson's tensile arms pumping;
legs wrapped and hugged tight
to his chest;
good marathon wheelchair form.
And grey Hinton, Alberta snow, falling.

THESE T.V. MEN AND WOMEN

These t.v. men and women people my life
with names like David and Joan,
Norm and Barbara and Oprah
and Johnny;
they smile and turn and move
in animated, air-brushed perfection
the glint and pouf and style
of each hair,
the sweep of a skirt,
taut and tight leg and neck and back,
the perfect eye
hands flutter bejewelled and multihued
by Revlon, Max Factor, L'Oreal, Maybelline.

These t.v. men and women;
passion and pain are fleeting in their perfection,
trauma is a 30-60-90-minute
rise and fall and test of
emotional reality/non-reality,
theirs and mine.
At arms-length, I am rich
and svelte and amorous and
tres, tres outre,
full of scandal and intrigue.
This vicarious multi-life we all
live and share with them
via channels and cable and
to-pay-or-not-to pay t.v.

To see the world in tiny bubbles
of early morning news shows
to bend and stretch and writhe
for twenty minutes 'round the clock
via cable;
to rend my heart by day or night-time soaps
to hold court with Phil or Oprah
or, to sit in on any number of
t.v. courtroom dramas

to cook and cook and cook
with Julia or some French or Creole chef
who allows the camera such intimacies
in his or her kitchen
to be history with PBS
which has made me Good Queen Bess
or some part of India or Africa
or even pre-history for 30 or 60 or 90 minutes.

I have seen the holocaust from many angles.

I examine South Africa again and again.
I, with billions of world viewers
exploded with the fated 1986 space shuttle
over and over and over again
as it disintegrated in a t.v. sky.

Oh, television
you chart and record my pre and current
and post history;
you are relentless in pursuit of my every
sleeping and waking hour.
Your people tattoo themselves on my life
in this surreal and glamorous
flicker and dim;
T.V.,
you orchestrate my life.

A KID MOVES THROUGH THE SYSTEM

A kid moves through the system
and deals with who
and when
and why
and what and when.
A kid moves through the system
and becomes the system
becomes bells and courses,
some subject level or other:
university prep
non-university prep
academic
honours
and otherwise
majors in cafeteria
or washroom
or at-the-fountain-as-often-as-possible
and, out of class lots
or in class, but, there-and-not-there.

A kid moves through the system —
a system which
shifts and changes and serves itself
by becoming curriculum-perfect
— a reflection of everyone else's
tried-and-true and then discarded system,
some American or Alberta
or some other place model
of the new look in education
which soon became the old look,

and then, not working,
became ours.

A kid moves through the system.

ADDENDUM

Addendum to Margaret Atwood's poem:
"Notes Toward A Poem That Can Never Be Written"

I read a poem to my class
about a poet who told the truth
about a poem that could not be written.
Her poem was only notes,
she said.
As we read through the poem
her truth billowing out before us
like well-filled sails
like the shocking pain of
white sails in the sun against our eyes.
Truth, like an ill-fitting, foot-thin dollar-rack shoe;
truth, like a soft linen or leather garment
married by years and comfort to your body;
truth and the poet
truth and my dreams
truth and my words.

You have left me with a dilemma, Margaret Atwood
left me to sift through the web of my words
my poems
which now, seem like notes
only notes
to the underground of me.

YOU, AND WORDS

You;
you make me move my pen
and draw a world of words across my page.
You turn your head and I see fields,
fields and streams and hills so green
and full of trees and cows
giving milk
giving words and poems
giving love.
You open wide your arms in love
and I write soft looks
soft touches and sweet smiles.
You, striding through my door,
through my life and through my heart
and I write bread and roses,
laughter and tears, and
a song that plays and plays in the heart-place.

THE BLUE WHALE HEART

The blue whale heart is as big as a Volkswagen.
Hearing this matter-of-fact on a PBS special
made me think of you
your heart so big and big
and giving;
moving over to make room for me
and the world;
your heart, raining cool and sweet
when my life is parched for strength.
Your heart, a feast of tension and passion
when I need to feel replete withal.
I could drive that blue whale Volkswagen-heart
right through yours.

SASKATCHEWAN SWEETGRASS DREAMS

I think of you tonight
far away in some Saskatchewan dreams,
the Montreal Lake Reserve which you
sleep on this night is as close as my atlas;
I find it: growing big and small and then
big again in the fake and portable clarity
of my magnifying glass.
I see you tonight,
sharing sweetgrass in some Cree's kitchen.
The west wind brings and shares it,
and you, with me
here, so far east,
away from you, and
cradling my atlas to keep you close.

OF YOU IN CANADA; OF ME IN VERMONT

Sumachs on the hillside
soft wash of Vermont sky sunset
clouds and sky pillow my mind
and my thoughts of you
as they soar and spiral
carried on piny mountain winds.

Cows on the hillside
leaves and trees and grassy meadow
pointillist living canvas
against the sky
like driving and living through a
Constable painting.

These Vermont winds cradle and caress me
as no man has, until you.
They are your caress,
so far away from me now.

This Vermont setting sun
makes me sepia, bronze,
burnished copper;
gives me the red-earth brown fire-skin
of my Micmac long ago.

Farms and hillsides rolling by
black and white cowscapes filling
my car window;
My eyes drink and drink
and drink their fill
of Vermont sun and sky and clouds
sending,
on these Vermont-to-Halifax winds
these words, and
my heartbeat.

DON'T GIVE ME LOOKS

Don't give me looks that put me in my place
that open my mail
that smell me coming and going, and see me everywhere.
Don't give me looks made of plastic smiles
reserved for co-workers who rush past
on a wave of caffeine and nicotine,
letting 'How are you?' drift and hang in the air.
You say, 'Fine!' neither hearing nor meaning it.
Don't give me those looks.
Don't give me looks full of hell and damn
and who cares? who cares?
that flap on the line like clothes in the wind
that ring and ring like a telephone in an empty room
that flicker white and snowy, like the telly at midnight
that are snowblind in August
that are full of all the rest of the world
and not me.

TO MEASURE DISTANCE AND DESIRE

Distance orchestrates my desire for you.
It ebbs and flows like a tide unwilling
to yield or be channelled.
This distance, this desire creates a language
for my solitude;
it speaks in the tongue of void
and with the lilting ache of being one.
I mark time by your absence.
My skin takes the measure of no touch;
no touch.
And always,
this orchestra, this crescendo,
this chorus
of this, my distant desire.

LOVE, THEY SAID

Hands,
he said.
Your hands
Your eyes
Your smile,
he said.
Skin,
she said.
Your skin
Your touch
Your breath
Your weight
Your sigh

Love, they said.
Our love.

ROSES OF WORDS

The pleasure is easy.
folding together
feeling/sharing warm and perfect and
man-woman whole world complete.
It's the other stuff that aches us, and
furrows our brows to seek and find
the words that whisper
and call and cry and define
my space
my life and need and vision;
making room for,
eclipsing you and all that you are.
These roses of words that come after pleasure,
that come between as push and pull
that perk and bulge and simmer and anger
that love and deny and break and
break and drift to compromise
like unwilling tide.

YOU IN MY TALK

my mind
my tongue betrays me now
rolling your name from my lips
in long-distance telephone talk
to my long-distance friend
who becomes your name too often in this conversation.
We're talking about me
my news and not news
my goods, my bads
my ups, my downs
my public brownie points
and my private failure which is you
you
your name drops among my words
flicks like a serpent's tongue toward my friend
this long-distant man who is friend and soul-mate
and knows me from my girlhood to now
in my cracked and imperfect womanhood.

too often
as this far-distant friend holds Ma Bell to his ear
to my MT&T admissions
of lingering love for you
of dreaming to you
of this, my latest mistake and assault of the heart
too often
this lovely man hears his own name become yours on my lips
over and over again.
until my *I'm sorries*
become part of the litany
of talking my hurt away
of calling him you
and almost calling him you
and talking
talking me strong
talking me back into
the big and Black and strong Maxine I really am.

BURY MY HEART BY DEGREES

Don't fall out of love in a small town like Halifax
restaurants
and rounding street corners
are deathtraps and
uncertain rendez-vous for old lovers;
one strong and flaunting heartlessness
and a new lover;
one is a shadow
and fragile
and trying to slip the skin of memory
but it fits too tight
parts cling
and grow back
and do not yield to picking at old wounds.

DISARMED AND DISBELIEVING

and James Taylor is singing '...ain't it good you've got a friend...'
but he's so wrong
we all know that
the lie hidden in those words
intoned with sincerity
on the night of early seduction
when I become a virgin again for you
when I become your lover
when I trust your words
when I am trapped by your lips
your touch
your arms and charms
and all of you, at once;
when I am disarmed
when you are with and without guile
when you speak and rehearse your apologies of the future
'I don't want to hurt you'
is a litany and curse and so, so fatalistic;
when I become the world
when the world is magic
when you and I are the best of all possible nights
when I am every sun and moon for you
when you are every star
when midnight never ends
when I am the violin eaten by the horse of Chagall
when you are the violin and I am the horse
when we are the end and the beginning
and the beginning again and again and again
when the beginning is my canvas
when joy is Van Gogh gold and pigment
and not those black blue skies
with burning swirls for stars;
when I become a virgin for you again
when I become your lover
when I am disarmed.

HEART UNDONE

Will I make that call?
Will I seal my fate? Ask you to dinner?
to a park bench; to a rendez, rendez-vous?
give you a chance to say No
give you a chance to skewer my heart
dice my desire
saute my fantasies
throw another heart on the barbie
get those unrequited flames going real good
get those coals to glowing embers
marshmallow-toast my heart like a happy camper;
trap my heart like some Radisson man
skin my heart like some leg-hold mink or rabbit;
tan and mount my heart like
moosehead antlers on the wall
label that trophy *Heart Undone*
bagged over and over again
you, cocked and armed for me
me, that heartbreak trophy waiting to be done in again
waiting to be on your wall
waiting.

JONI MITCHELL AGAIN

I'm listening to Joni Mitchell again
listening to
this blonde and thin
opposite-to-me
Canadian singer-woman that she is
listening to her
sing those songs of broken hearts and love
lost, stolen or strayed that I am
singing my heart.

I'm listening to Joni Mitchell again
like I did
after the first time
and then, after every
harsh and loveless
surgery of the heart.
I know that I'm weak and strong at the same time now
that the endless smile shrouds the nicks and wounds,
incisions which live, and
gape open under the surface of me.

I'm listening to Joni Mitchell again.
cranking it up
filling my life with her silver and healing voice
when the hurt is like a heartbeat;
Just playing Joni Mitchell music
low and constant
when I'm feeling strong
but need her watercolour sounds
around me when I look up,
like the comfort of Monet;
that colour, non-colour
womb-sea of escape that is his.

I'm listening to Joni Mitchell again
listening to her save her own life
listening to her chart
and save mine.

TO SAY THAT THIS IS THE END

To say that this is the end
To give up the fantasy that
dreams are really you, and
that every telephone ring will be you.
I would be the svelte woman on
every high fashion runway.
I would be Sally Ride in space.
I would be the snowflake hot-and-cold
on the tongue
the sleek and deadly shark sifting
through currents
the Ben Johnson impulse to run/fly
the Karen Kain pas de deux
the 'get up - stand up' Bob Marley reggae line.
I would be the shimmer of light and colour
through shot silk
the perfect ebb and flow of tide and time
the thought of a kiss, and
the afterthought.
To be so wise and blessed with
logic and desire and a heart that
knew just when to stop.

II. Black Song Nova Scotia

RACISM

Racism:
the alphabet of that word
a metallic absurdity on the tongue
the cell of its imprisonment
slamming down all of your days
on all of your life.

The cage of racism
allowing no life-to-life cross-over
to the other side
no people to people
mind to mind
heart to heart.

The bite of racism
is deep and deep
and relentless in its pursuit
incising Black and Native and language and
gender cultures
excising the heart of all that we are.

We bleed generations of pain.
We heal to hope.
We rise to challenge.
We shout the imperative.
We stride the future.

The language of the Black and Native future
has no alphabet for racism,
has no agenda for it
no taste
no time
no reality.

And in some future Black and Native time
the rain of racism falls
and finds no waiting hearts,
finds no ground wanting.

AFRICVILLE SPIRIT

I am Maxine Tynes.
I am not from Africville, born and bred.
But Tynes is a Black Community name
and I am from this community;
this Maritime, Halifax, down home Nova Scotia Black community.
And so as a kid growing up in Dartmouth
in the Black four or five generations Tynes homestead
of my parents Joe Tynes and Ada Maxwell Tynes
I grew up knowing about Africville and hearing
of Africville through the family talks
and from the Africville friends of my own folks.
I believe what I learned at home
and what I say and insist to my students and to any audience:
that it is important to recognize
Black community and to own community and all Black experience.
That there are no borders, no boundaries, no frontiers that matter
in the Diaspora, in this North American,
Western world Black reality.
That the 49th Parallel or the Atlantic Ocean or the Pacific
does not matter or make a difference.
To people of colour, oppression is oppression.
That disenfranchisement
and racism is the same everywhere.
That Soweto is Chicago is Toronto
is Detroit is Montreal is New York is Halifax and Dartmouth is
Africville.

AFRICVILLE IS MY NAME
The great Black American writer, James Baldwin said:
"If you don't know my name, then you don't know your own."

Personhood; Nationhood, Statehood; Community; Family;
Personhood.
To own one's community.
To voice its name with history and with pride.
To map that community with a litany of community names.
To raise the profile of that community,
again and again.
To etch Africville into the Past, the Present, and relentlessly
into the Future.
To sing, to say, to shout the names of Africville like a map,
like a litany, like a hymn and a battle-cry,
like a flag and a constitution,
like a banner of the Africville that was, that is,
that always will be;

First Black Settlers: William Brown, John Brown, Thomas Brown

Alcock	Alexander	Anderson
Berryman	Bowels	Brown
Byers	Carter	Carvery
Cassidy	Desmond	Dixon
Downey	Emmerson	Farrell
Ferguson	Fletcher	Flint
Gannon	Grant	Hamilton
Howe	Izzard	Johnson
Jones	Kane	Keelor
Kellom	Lawrence	MacDonald
Mantley	Maree	Marsman
Medley	Mewman	Nichols
Pannell	Parris	Perry
Roan	Skinner	Sparks
Steed	Stewart	Thomas
Tollivar	Wareham	Wearry
Wilcox	West	Williams
Vemb		

Personhood. Community. Family. Africville.

AFRICVILLE

We are Africville
we are the dispossessed Black of the land
creeping with shadows
with life
with pride
with memories
into the place made for us
creeping with pain away from our home
carrying, always carrying
Africville on our backs
in our hearts
in the face of our child and our anger.

I am Africville
says a woman, child, man at the homestead site.
This park is green; but
Black, so Black with community.
I talk Africville
to you
and to you
until it is both you and me
till it stands and lives again
till you face and see and stand
on its life and its forever
Black past.

No house is Africville.
No road, no tree, no well.
Africville is man/woman/child
in the street and heart Black Halifax,
the Prestons, Toronto.

Wherever we are, Africville,
you and we are that Blackpast homeground.
We mourn for the burial of our houses, our church, our roads;
but we wear Our Africville face and skin and heart.
For all the world.
For Africville.

BLACK SONG NOVA SCOTIA

We are Africville and Preston,
North and East
We are Portia White singing to a long-ago king
We are Edith Clayton weaving the basketsong of life
Black and old with history
and strong with the new imperative.
We are Graham Jarvis bleeding on the road in Weymouth Falls.
We are the Black and the invisible
We are here and not here
We are gone but never leave
We have voice and heart and wisdom
We are here
We are here
We are here.

ON LEARNING THAT I MIGHT HAVE INDIAN BLOOD

My mother's nose makes sense to me now
and all of those cheekbones
mine (when I'm thinner)
my brother Pete's
and Aunt Lillian's;
the face bones of some long-ago
first-walker of this North American soil
Micmac — somehow sideways or
straight up-and-down undocumented
ancestor or other
and Grandfather Dave Maxwell
locked and frozen in that photograph,
eyes piercing me forever through the
relentless clarity of old photo-face
Indian, through you to me.

So that's what those eyes that stare,
that thin little defiant man-face of yours
has been saying and showing to me
when I pass you and I see you, and I don't
in that hall
on that wall.

You say: girl
you ain't got those cheeks for nothin'.

Pick some chieftain (male or female)
from the Micmac pages of your past;
call his
call her name right out loud
say it
and say it
and say it
'til it fits and feels like eelskin
'til it pricks like quills
'till it burns and smells and smells
like sweetgrass

then, wear it all the ways that you will:
as your name
as a poem
as a song
as a coat of many feathers and colours
as the kiss, the touch, the breath of a lover
as your Dave, Ada, some long-ago Indian Maxwell
as your window, door, key to the past wherever
so your skin in summer is no puzzle when it goes copper
so your past is no longer a mystery
so you can make your own folklore up
so you can savour your private affinity with the First People
because you were there, too;

so you can sniff the winter, spring, rain-fresh
night-time sea or morning air more knowingly
and your mother's nose can make more sense to you now.
And in some future then
you can say and revel in exactly why.

AFRICA IN THE WORLD

Written to Commemorate the opening: VISUAL VARIATIONS/AFRICAN
WORLDS , Dalhousie University Art Gallery, September 8, 1988.

I am Africa in the world.
I cast my shadow long and wide and Black and everywhere
and green is my flag of the earth
and red is the bloodline from here to there;
it is said that you all share the beat of my blood.
A powerful legacy.

This daughter of the Nile, Limpopo, Sudan, Zaire, Zambezi, Senegal
and Zimbabwe
walks the Diaspora;
I talk Africa.
I walk with her rhythm and her strength.
I shout Africa when I give you my profile.

Look carefully with Western eyes to see my neck-coils,
my coiled and adorned hair
my face tattooed and coloured with the earth,
the birds, the sky;
my arms clack with bracelets of baobab and cowrie,
my foot-dress is the dust of the Serengeti.

I see with you, here, my icons.

This sweetmeat face-mask fills my eye, Africa,
and I am happy.
This persimmon bittersweet image bites my eye
and Africa, I am found.

Face of this mother-continent
with your full lips speaking Kikuyu, Swahili, Shona,
Ndebele, Tswana, Xhosa, Zulu, Yoruba, Ibo, Hausa
in rich savannah
across these Benin, Yoruba, Serengeti dreams
Serengeti dreams
Serengeti dreams
my neck coils

my breastplate
my talking
talking
talking stick
my mango, and
my breadfruit

I did not know what 'heavy' was and is
until I lifted these sights and sounds and images
of old Africa to my mind.

This estuary of image and shape and colour,
round and round
that we stand on
this bridge that is
this space that is
this time that is here and now
Africa, and all of us.

I am Africa in the world.

RACISM ... TO RAISE THE HEART AGAINST

The hue and cry of racism
tears at every mother's heart
wreaks havoc on the guard of the fathers' heart
treads hard upon the path of childhood
blinds young eyes to the wealth of life
to the colour spectrum that is human.

The language of racism breaks on the tongue
breaks the tongue that tries love and compassion
speaks in limits and exclusion
inhales the ash of distrust
exhales the acid breath of hate.
The body of racism
a rancid, bloated wreck
adrift on the flotsam sea of humankind at waste
the offal of misguidance at the hearth; in the cradle
the misshapen product of the womb of hatred
the stench of the bigot charred and charred on the flame of racism.

Bury the flesh, the bones, the vessel of racism
inter the carrion of life's heart
sink it deep and deep
and deep to some place of nothing
plumb the depths of nowhere, to some nth of nothing
to some nth of nothing
nothing left
nothing wanting
no ground in which to plant and start the seed of racism
no root to grow
no green place of love and nurture
except for all that we,
who walk the path of good and hope and sweet,
sweet possibility,
are to each other.

We hear the sweep and call of sisterhood; of brotherhood.
We heed that call.
We dance the pace and measure of peace in the heart.

THE CALL TO TEA

To commemorate Portia White, classically trained operatic singer of great international reputation during the 1940s. A great Black Maritime woman.

The call to tea
a solid knell of the social register
in old Halifax
silk moire
dank velvet
crepe and lace splayed across settee
mahogany and divan
the shadow of servers
invisible in stiff black stuff
laying table
just so, with the delicacy of
cucumber, tea-cake and scone
on porcelain and silver
filigree of lacy oak leaf shadow
through a southend Halifax window.

To be so owned and distanced
to be called to tea
to have opened that dark and silver throat
and poured sweet amber liquid
upon the crowned heads of England
and of Europe and left them wanting;
to have New York and great Carnegie
glittering and applauding behind and
around and ever after that dusky
dusky throat.

To be so owned and distanced
to be called to tea
Miss W____,
so dusky proud and unassuming
to own and execute that throat of miracles
to sit, owned and distanced,
this daughter of old Halifax
this feted lady of the world stage
to feel the shudder of upscale lashes seeking presence

denying connection
translucent skin retracting
peeling back vacant smiles
the hollow ring of truth not spoken
this parody of social tea
oak shadows filigreed and fallen
through prestigious southend window

The tea, finding path down and
down that dusky throat
the elixir of that moment
poured so elegantly by some pale and glittering I.O.D.E. arm.

To be so owned and distanced
to be called to tea in genteel Halifax
of that era
so fresh from singing to some king,
some prince or president.

Later, one of them would say,
"It was so hard not to ask her to go down to the cellar
to fetch a scuttle of coal."

III. The Portrait Poems

1. SERENGETI SMILE

For Rosemary, who painted my life.

Lady fingers
Lady Lady colour-fingers
you have painted the suns and
the moons of Africa
into my eyes, and
into my life
my skin shouts Africa
under your touch of red black azure plum sungold
the lapis of my eyes and lips
the Serengeti of my smile
Lady colour-fingers
we laugh and we are women
and you release the Zaire soul of me.

2. THE TALK OF THE SITTING

The talk of the sitting
the banter between strokes on canvas
it lulls and it incites colour and mute:

Oh, your ears
Those eyes... Are they your mother's?
Grandmother Nellie's cheekbones
That's my Dad's dimple.
He claimed it for his own
every time he'd bite my nose
to make me laugh.

You uncover and uncover so much,
artist, with your probing talk
and talk and colourplay.

3. COLOUR-STRUCK

on canvas
my body rolls in palette splendour
my pores sing rainbows
my heart takes wing
and dances sunrise, sunset Zambezi fire.

4. WHEN THE SETTING IS MY CLASSROOM

then I am all of my Blackest self
artist, darken your palette
black the to and fro of me
make black punctuation
of all of my dimensions
the crook of my arm, a sleek
black comma
we will go on and on and on
my eyes, the end point of exclamation
I black the air with the rush of
words from my lips
artist, artist, make ebony your brush
canvas black me to the world.

5. THE PORTRAIT SPEAKS AND SOARS AND FLARES IN BIG COLOUR

this woman who is me on canvas
burgeoning colour and life and
womanself, so big and big
and big in light and shadow
this woman
Gauguin bright and splendour
greening and growing in all of the reds
the golds, and black and violet shimmer of life

this canvas cannot hold her passion
her worlds and worlds of
words and laughter

she swims and pushes out to me
through strokes of pigment

she is big and bigger than me in life
she fills my heart and my eyes
the black and colour of her
arrests me in the heartplace of my chest

a new full and hollow thump is there

I know that forever now
her big-hued embrace waits for me
in that room, from that wall

My Daddy Joe would say 'Heavenly Days!'
my Mama Ada would say: MAXINE!
                         MAXINE!
                         MAXINE!

6. AGAINST A WALL, SMILING

I am furled against a wall
my dress, like a golden wave around me
I am smiling
I feel like a door permanently ajar.

IV. Stories

HELEN AND THE EVERYNIGHT SING-SONG

Those were the nights that were very special. Those nights that happened and were full of songs and Helen and my brothers and sisters and me. Those nights that often were Friday nights or Saturday nights or any old day of the week night. Those were the nights when we would sing for Helen. Those were the nights that were so special to all of us. All of the stair-step kids in that little brown house.

Mama's lady-friend, Helen, would be there in our squashy little railroad station-like kitchen, so long and narrow and lined all along one yellow wall with chairs. There she would be, in her big tan or navy blue coat, all fluffed out around her, in her velvet tam and perfumy Juicy Fruit gum, having tea with our Mama.

We'd peek out from the pantry or from the dining room door and see. Mama and Helen talking. Or not talking. It was really important to see all of that. Helen and Mama talking meant it wasn't time yet for us to be there. But as soon as Mama disappeared into the dishes or ironing or one of the little brown babies, and Helen disappeared into the newspaper until only the fuzzy red or gold top of her tam could be seen, then we knew. And we looked and giggled and told each other to "Come on. Let's sing for Helen."

And sing we did. The whole little motley crew of us would one by one, or in bolder two by twos, sidle up to our Helen. This everynight lady in our house who was not our auntie or cousin or anything like that. But she was every bit as much ours as all of that, or maybe even more so, in spite of it.

Anyway, we didn't care. We were going to sing for her. I would sidle up to her, to sneak a cherished rub of that velvet tam, and to say those magic everynight words: "Want us to sing for you, Helen?"

I know now, looking back from the steep hill of adulthood, that those truly were the magic words.

"Want us to sing for you, Helen?"

To have asked for permission, to have said, "May we sing for you?" would have guaranteed a response not from Helen but from our Mama who would have appeared from behind her camouflage of ironing to have said any one of her hundreds of ever-ready noes, with any one of those hundreds of mother-reasons attached. Like, "It's too late." "It's bedtime. You're bothering Helen. She came here for a little peace." But we knew the magic — the kid magic of what to say to make things happen.

"Want us to sing for you, Helen?"

The old grey head would raise up to give me a nod and a smile.

"Hi, girlie. Want to sing for Helen?"

Oh, the joy of it! By this time I'd be standing close. Babbling away. Saying that I'd learned a new song in school that day. Asking Helen if she wanted to hear it.

The old grey head would be nodding and smiling. Blue or tan coat arms would be folding up the newspaper, and oh, the clouds of Juicy Fruit that seemed to surround her would be like some heady charm to me. Helen would pull me in close to her.

"Come on, girlie. Sing for Helen."

And I would. I'd shove my little brown self up close to her to breathe in all the Juicy Fruit warmth of her. I'd throw back my head and sing and sing for all my little brown might. And one by one, all of my little stair-step brothers and sisters would sidle up and soon we were a chorus. Four or five sweet-child voices raised in smooth or ragged song.

There we were every night. Shout-singing all kinds of songs, in and out of harmony. Summer songs. Blue bird and black bird songs.

82

Sleeptime songs. School songs. Even camp songs of camps we never went to. We'd sing-shout them all. All of those young voices singing loudly and happily. Completely without guile. Wagging our heads and being close to our Helen. The everynight sing-song.

And where was our Mama in all of this? Well, she was there, to be sure. Like all mothers then, our Mama was always there. Maybe the everynight sing-song was for her, too. Something she got but didn't have to bargain for, organize or agree to.

After all, we used the kid-magic to ask Helen if she wanted us to sing for her. And our Helen always said yes. What could Mama do or say to stop it? Perhaps she never wanted to anyway.

Because there we all were, the last half of her sizeable brood, singing and doing her proud. The wagging little girl heads, crinkly black braids sticking straight up and out and not moving an inch. The sturdy little and bigger brothers, brown arms dangling out of t-shirts and plaid shirts, pumping to the sing-song melodies or sneaking in a pinch or poke or a tug on one of the crinkly braids.

I'm sure Mama watched us. Perhaps she even slowed her kitchen work while we sang. Perhaps, though, she bustled about in her usual brisk way, our singing a buoyant cushion of new energy for her each night.

And at the end of it all, she'd end our impromptu serenade with: "That's enough now, children. Say good-night to Helen."
And she'd watch us each accept our treasured half-stick of the prized and fragrant Juicy Fruit Gum from our Helen as she praised our efforts and bid us good-night.

"That was nice, children," she'd say. "Good night."

"Night, Helen," we'd all chorus.

"What do you say, children?" Mama would prompt us.

"Thank you, Helen," came the chorus.

"You're welcome, children. Good night."

So sweet and so formal we all were at the end.

Often I would hang back to lean in close, close, close — to kiss that old, worn cheek. There was always the surprise of sinking into all of the warm, sweet fragrance of her.

"Thank you, girlie. 'Night now."

Our Helen. She felt soft and warm and always smelled of Juicy Fruit Gum.

FOR TEA AND NOT FOR SERVICE

The ticking of the clock was like a heartbeat in that oh so correct and perfect room. That Southend parlour, so well appointed with its fullness of oak and plush velvet and its surround of windows heavy with lace.

There she sat. Small and dark and such a counter-point to everything around her today in this room, in this house, with these people. These pale women.

The Imperial Daughters had asked Celie to tea. And so she had come to tea. After the surprise of the invitation and the rounds and rounds of talk at home about that invitation, Celie had come to the Imperial Daughters' tea. A small smile as she replayed the at-home talk about the invitation. Even the white vellum card had been weighed, passed from one worn, dark hand to another. She had assured her folks that, yes, indeed, that ragged creamy edge was as it should be, a sign of value and quality and not discard paper. Even the handwriting, black and elaborate like bits of some insect's wings, had been scrutinized and remarked over.

"Hmph! Would you look at that! Couldn't even send your invite on decent paper. Looks torn out of somethin' to me."

That was Celie's mother. And some variation of the same was offered by the aunts and the others until Celie assured them that, no, this was indeed some good, heavy white vellum notepaper, complete with watermark — showing them how to look for it — and probably from the Boston States.

Celie smiled at this. No wonder she felt ready for everything all the time, with that dark circle ever-present, hovering to protect her with love and the defiance of talk at home.

"Celie, dear...? Is everything all right?" Mrs. Browne-Thorne. The lady of the house. Fluttering around her now like her nickname. "Birdie" Browne-Thorne, the hostess of the Celie Harris Imperial Daughters' Tea.

Celie looked into that figure of ivory lace and dove-grey watered silk and considered the question.

Is everything all right? Well, let's see now. Yes, she was Celie Harris, Halifax's own international songstress of the operatic stage. Yes, she was here by invitation. Yes, she was seated at tea in this Southend parlour-shrine of oak and velvet affluence. There were no more yesses.

No one had come near the small, dark woman since her arrival. Oh, she had been shown into the tea-room, the parlour by her hostess, and seated comfortably enough. The tea-cup was of adequately fine China and the tea-cakes sufficiently dainty, with their companion crustless and anaemic cucumber finger sandwiches, all by her side. The perfect Southend Halifax formal tea picture. Except that not one of the Imperial Daughters had spoken to their dusky guest of honour since her arrival. Instead, they fluttered among themselves, just out of reach. A corner of the storm and flurry of fine lace and brocade and the patina of old pearls against white throats.

Celie raised her eyes to Mrs. Browne-Thorne's uncertain gaze. No words came.

"Fine, dear. Fine. Fine." The bird-like flutter of hands at the crepey throat. She fled. Back to the reluctant flock, so Celie thought.

Why had they asked her here if they weren't wanting to talk to her? But Celie knew even before the thought was complete. She knew only too well how high her stock was on the social register; at least her name was. Celie Harris, Black girl out of Halifax who sings for Europe and for crowned heads of state and even fills Carnegie Hall with her strong and dusky voice. Celie knew that here at home her name was the prize on the invitation that would be multiplied in the weekend Gazetteer. Her name was of sufficient credit that it would shore up Birdie Browne-Thorne's Southend status. Her name was fine. It was the flag that bannered her art, her music, her song, her celebrity.

Another shadow approaching now. Celie immediately let out that breath from deep in her chest as she recognized the shadow as Dora Skyke from "out home." Mama had reminded her to keep an eye out for Dora. That Dora would look after her here. After all, this was Dora's "place." Her live-in place with the Browne-Thornes for as long as Celie could remember. And longer.

My, didn't Dora look all crisp and stiff and black and white? Bigger somehow than she looked to Celie at church. Anyway, didn't she just own this place, the way she moved in it? Better than Birdie Browne-Thorne herself.

Bit quiet she was, though, here. None of that hearty head-back bellowing laugh of hers that just rang through the Cheapside Market on the week-end mornings. No big "Hey, you-gal!" from Dora in this room. Just that efficient black shadow coming and going. Celie was glad just to see her in that room anyway, that seemed to be growing bigger by the minute.

Dora caught Celie's eye just then and the two women looked closely and warmly into each other, and each felt at home in the other's gaze. Celie caught Dora's broad smile, flashing those gaps in front, and she purely did feel better, almost herself again.

Funny, but she'd wondered and, yes, even worried over knowing she would see Dora here. Celie thought for sure she'd be feeling all hot and just awful at this moment, when Dora would be handing her tea and cakes and looking after her as if she was white. She didn't want to have that happen, but of course it did ... the thing was, though, Celie felt all right there with Dora. Dora wasn't feeling at all bad about it. Celie could tell. And at least Dora wasn't pretending that she wasn't there.

Dora was gone. Not really. Just being a shadow again. Black and silent and efficient, bearing tea-cakes to and fro among the Imperial Daughters.

There they all were. Fluffed into clumps and clusters on the settees and such around the perimeter of this room. The talk was low and strained. Well-coiffed heads dipped to shield eyes that stole her way to take the measure of Celie and to record — incredulously — her presence in that pre World War Two room among Halifax gentlewomen.

That clock ticked like a wanton heartbeat.

Celie sat and stiffened and felt her throat; her lovely, lovely throat of musical miracles constrict.

"Why am I here? Why did I come to this farce of a tea? Do they want me here? They want my name. Why don't they talk to me? Ask me something — anything. About Europe. About Carnegie Hall. Anything."

Ah, but Celie knew. They wanted her name. On the social page. High up. Listed conspicuously with theirs. Imperial Daughters of Halifax had Celie Harris to tea as the guest of Mrs. Birdie Browne-Thorne of Young Avenue.

Celie doesn't remember the afternoon ending, or how she got out of there. But she does remember the warm and secret hug from Dora as she put Celie into her coat; and that hot, breathy whisper into Celie's collar, " I knows 'em, child. I knows 'em too well."

The story that Celie took home to her Mama was an artful fabrication of the gaiety of the afternoon, the talks and the camaraderie that she had been drawn into. Mama Harris was happy with that story. Celie's celebrated throat ached and burned while she told it. All lies. And then it was forgotten. Put away where it couldn't trip her as she continued on the exquisite road to acclaim for her voice — the acclaim that was to be hers, both afar and at home, long after that incredible afternoon.

Years later, Celie heard that Dora had left her live-in place with Birdie Browne-Thorne. Quit was the story that Dora told whenever pressed. But there is always something else.

Seems that one of the dowagers of the deep Southend proclaimed to all and sundry that afternoon that, celebrated songstress or not, she could barely abide being to tea with "that gal." And how could Birdie Browne? In fact, as she said or boasted. "It was all I could do to keep from asking that gal to go down to the cellar to fetch a scuttle of coal."

Well it seems that the wrong ears heard; Dora's of course. It also seems that the lady in question went home with coal dust dumped liberally — somehow — into the folds and recesses of her wraps. And once the story got told at the Cheapside Market, complete with mime and that trademark head-thrown-back laugh, Dora soon left Birdie Browne-Thorne's service.

Knowing that years later, Celie allowed the memories of that awful tea party to come back at odd moments; especially in those tight moments before she stepped into some spotlight to open that sweet and dusky throat.

The memories are strong and urgent and filled with Dora's smile and with the ticking heartbeat of the clock in that genteel room.

THOSE LOOKS

Maddie began to think about the looks she was getting. And she began to feel them. In her mouth, like hard candies that refuse to get soft and sweet.

They weren't even looks at a part of her body — the kind of looks that women are suspicious of and are aware of in the most unlikely circumstances and from the most unlikely of people. Maddie knew those looks. All women got them. No. These were not those kinds of looks.

They were the looks that got in under Maddie's hair and in under her eyelids and sifted through her. Questioning looks, probing in their silence. Louder than a shout. Looks that said, "Why are you Maddie, instead of Madeline?" to everyone. And why Madeline when most girls and women are Heather or Sarah or Lisa or Michelle, or some movie or day-time soap opera star's name?

Madeline. She was never Madeline. Only on all of her remembered first-days-of-school when some well-meaning, well-groomed new teacher would intone, "Madeline?" with a question mark behind it to see who would answer.

"Maddie" would be her quiet reply. Not "Here." Not "Present." Just "Maddie." And that was that.

Maddie shifted in her seat. She could feel the lift and roll of the harbour under the boat. She felt good in the slowed-down fifteen minutes it took for the ferry crossing.

She shifted. She looked out at the constant gulls wheeling and calling in the distance over the oil rig tied up at the Dartmouth Marine Slips. Maddie felt her sweater begin to prickle under her arms. She felt hot and dark. She knew that when she took her sweater off later, the neck-band would be damp and sour-smelling.

Sitting there, feeling good being on the ferry, Maddie was glad she'd remembered to wear her sunglasses. Hidden behind them, she took stock of the other passengers. A few women alone. Some women with women-friends or man-friends. A couple of groups of three or four teenagers. A scattering of men alone on the ferry. Typical ferryboat crowd. Nothing interesting about them. Not like her. Everybody knew her. Or pretended like they did. Or acted like it. Or wanted to.

Maddie had discovered that once your face is on a magazine cover, even in a small town like hers, your privacy slowly, then suddenly, is gone.

So now there were the looks. Looks that seemed to smell her coming and going. That lay in wait for her to round a street corner. To enter a room. Looks that alternately invited and retreated, that praised and appraised. Looks that were like traps.

Often the looks became voices carried on lips and breath up close to her.

"Aren't you...? I know you... Tell me ... Excuse me, but..."

"Excuse me but..."

What? Oh, This one is real. It's not saying it knows me, or reads me. It's saying something real.

"The boat's in. You'll have to get off now."

That's o.k. Maddie knows that people expect people like her to act funny sometimes. Writers and artists are like that.

Acting funny is what her family called it, what her brothers and sisters teased her about back then.

"Maddie's acting funny again."

91

But Maddie knew what it was, this "acting funny." They saw her in those odd moments which became more and more frequent over time — those moments when some new or wonderful or big idea would begin perking in that young writer's head of hers. They saw her here-and-not-here in those moments, hands idling in cold dishwater while an impatient sister chattered on, waiting to dry, eager to fly away from chores. Or her mother would catch her hands idle in a tangle of some small sister's hair in the midst of braiding that black and wiry stuff.

"Maddie! Where are you, girl? You're not here, that's for sure. Keep your mind on what you're doing. You move like cold molasses! That child wants to get to bed sometime tonight. And you day-dreaming!"

That's right. *Here and not here.* Maddie knew. Those were the where and when her writer's thoughts, her poet's thoughts began.

Those beginnings were so real and so unreal at the same time. How could she tell them to her mother. Or to anyone? She could barely tell them to herself.

Everything around her faded to slightly out-of-focus when those moments hit. Of course, her mother was right. Maddie was "here and not here" most of the time. Most of her, the Maddie that was all thoughts and tingling nerve endings, was looking into the writer and poet part of her.

In those moments she was stepping, then walking, even running through the world of thoughts and half-thoughts; so nebulous but real and powerful enough to become words and poems later, even days and days later. Maddie knew she carried those thoughts inside her head like sweet and silent treasures. Sometimes they shone from her eyes in the sparks that made her eyes smile. Sometimes she would be smiling broadly, tickled or otherwise touched by those sweet and secret thoughts waiting to be poems. A classic Maddie moment in her memory. It could happen when she was elbow-deep in slightly gelled dishwater, blissfully staring into the middle-distance with that smile.

92

Being all of that in that small, overcrowded, growing-up house; overflowing with big and little kids, toys, books everywhere, and laundry baskets full-then-empty and clothes always full-bodied with the harbour wind, flapping and soaring on the line. Maddie "being funny again" was in full view and on target.

"Maddie, smiling like a Cheshire cat again! Change that water. Get those dishes done. Time's going." That was Mama. Did she know? Couldn't she feel all that heat and throbbing insistence that beat inside Maddie's head and ...

Crack! The snapping of the wet tea towel was like a bite and slap on her arm. Little sister.

"Oww! Hey! What did you do that for?"

"Because you're just standin' there with that dopey-dopey look on your face, that's why. And I want to go out before it gets dark, that's why." The impatient little sister.

"And Mama said you have to finish them yourself, slow-poke." She was gone.

Maddie barely said goodbye. The full-of-wind clothes flapping outside the window were like sentinels to her and that crowd of thoughts. The marauding crowd which dropped like inky birds onto her page becoming lines and poems.

Love and peace. The kitchen grew dark. Maddie and the water stood cold. The clothes line people flapped and stood watch outside the kitchen window. The thoughts inside her head grew and became a horde.

"Miss? I say, Miss?"

Someone was shaking her.

"Are you getting off? The boat's in. You'll have to get off and pay again if you're staying on for the ride back to Dartmouth."

93

The uniform loomed over her, startling Maddie back, out of her reverie so familiar.

"Oh. No, thanks. I'm off. Thanks."

She looked at him. Above that red and bristling moustache, this man who was a stranger, rousing her from her thoughts, was looking at her with the same look she got from folks at home so long ago. Wondering if she was all there at that moment. Wondering where her mind had been. Maddie knew. She smiled from her eyes, letting them reassure him. She reached for her companion cane but he was already handing it to her. Maddie knew that people were waiting to get on the ferry. Nobody could get on until everyone was off. Halifax folks, she thought. Let 'em wait. That made a laugh bubble right out of her. What would he think now?

A quick check of her overflowing Kenya bag for her book of poetry and her manuscript notebooks. Yes. Hat on. Scarf. Yes. All set. And the sunglasses. Maddie moved now, cane thumping, head down watching her step as she left the boat. Just enough time to make it to the gallery for her reading.

A pluck on her sleeve; a hand on her arm, stopping her. The strange and familiar face up close.

"Excuse me, but... Aren't you...?"